Spotlight on™
Reading
Comprehension

Characters
and
Actions

Linda Bowers
Rosemary Huisingh
Paul Johnson
Carolyn LoGiudice
Jane Orman

Skill Areas: Reading Comprehension
              Main Idea and Details
              Vocabulary and Semantics
              Characters and Actions
              Asking Questions
              Writing
Ages: 7 through 10
Grades: 2 through 5

LinguiSystems®

LinguiSystems, Inc.
3100 4th Avenue
East Moline, IL 61244-9700

FAX: 800-577-4555
E-mail: service@linguisystems.com
Web: linguisystems.com

800-776-4332

Copyright © 2005 LinguiSystems, Inc.

Printed in the U.S.A.

ISBN 0-7606-0583-1

About the Authors

From the left: Rosemary Huisingh, Jane Orman, Paul Johnson, Carolyn LoGiudice, Linda Bowers

Our lively team of speech-language pathologists and educators includes LinguiSystems owners and employees. We collaborated to develop *Story Comprehension To Go* in 2003. In response to customer requests for more materials with this approach to reading comprehension, we created this series of six books in a new *Spotlight on Reading Comprehension* series:

Characters and Actions

Comparing and Contrasting

Figurative Language and Exclusion

Making Inferences and Drawing Conclusions

Paraphrasing and Summarizing

Sequencing and Problem Solving

Together we have many years of experience in working with students to boost their language, thinking, and reading skills. We share a zest for life and a passion for high-quality instruction for all students. We hope the materials we present reflect our philosophy.

Illustrations by Margaret Warner

Cover design by Mike Paustian

Table of Contents

Introduction

Story Comprehension To Go was developed in 2003 for students in grades two through five, especially those who have difficulty with reading comprehension tasks. It includes numerous brief reading passages with reading comprehension questions for each one. This resource highlights essential reading comprehension tasks, including these:

Detecting the Main Idea
Recalling Details
Vocabulary and Semantics
Comparing and Contrasting
Exclusion
Problem Solving
Characters and Actions

Figurative Language
Predicting
Making Inferences
Drawing Conclusions
Paraphrasing
Summarizing

Due to the popularity of *Story Comprehension To Go*, we developed six booklets as sequels in a *Spotlight on Reading Comprehension* series. Each booklet includes stories and comprehension questions for detecting the main idea, identifying details, and thinking about the vocabulary and semantics. In addition, each booklet includes comprehension questions for a specific skill area. This particular booklet features questions that require students to understand the characters and their actions in the stories. The other five booklets are these:

Comparing and Contrasting
Making Inferences and Drawing Conclusions
Paraphrasing and Summarizing
Sequencing and Problem Solving
Figurative Language and Exclusion

The readability of the passages is controlled, based on the Flesch-Kincaid readability statistics. These statistics were revised in 2002; the new statistics yield a higher grade level in most cases than the previous ones. The range in readability is from grade levels 2.0 through 4.9. Each booklet includes eleven passages with the following readability ranges:

Passages 1-3   Readability 2.0-2.9

Passages 4-7   Readability 3.0-3.9

Passages 8-11   Readability 4.0-4.9

The question pages for each passage also ask students to formulate questions about what they have read. The last task for each passage is a related writing prompt.

Use these passages for groups of students or individuals. Photocopy or print the material from the CD so each student has a copy. Encourage your students to highlight or underline key information as they read each passage and to jot down any questions they have.

Research proves that repeated readings improve reading comprehension and that three readings are usually sufficient repetition for a student to grasp the content, assuming a passage is at or below the student's reading competency level. We recommend training students to read a passage three times for adequate comprehension before trying to answer the comprehension questions.

The reading comprehension questions are similar to those found on classroom and national reading comprehension tests. Have your students read each possible answer for the multiple-choice questions before they select their answers.

The answers for most of the comprehension questions are listed in the answer key on page 40. In some cases, the answers are just examples of appropriate responses. Accept all logical responses as correct.

As you present this information to your students, model your own reading comprehension strategies. Talk about ways to rescan a passage to find key information and other tips that will help your students improve their reading competence and confidence.

We hope you will find this book a welcome resource to help students understand and find satisfaction in what they read.

Linda, Rosemary, Paul, Carolyn, and Jane

Story 1

Everyone in Jon's family has a job to do at mealtime. Mom and Dad get the food ready. Brenda sets the table. Jed and Mike do the dishes. Jon's job is to feed Max, the dog.

When Jon got to the table, his place was not set. "Where's my plate?" he asked.

"You didn't feed Max today," said Mom. "This is the third time this week you didn't feed Max. Max was hungry. You need to learn a lesson. You may sit with us while we eat. You can think about your job and Max. You can think about being hungry. After we eat, you may have your dinner."

Main Idea and Details

1. What is the main idea of this story?

   a. Everyone has a job to do.

   b. Mom and Dad get the food ready.

   c. Brenda sets the table.

2. What was Jon's job?

   a. Jon's job was to clean up.

   b. Jon's job was to walk the dog.

   c. Jon's job was to feed the dog.

3. Who is Max?

   a. Max is Jon's sister.

   b. Max is Jon's dog.

   c. Max is Jon's brother.

Vocabulary and Semantics

4. Brenda set the table. What does **set the table** mean?

   a. Put the chairs around the table.

   b. Put the pans on the table.

   c. Put the dishes and silverware on the table.

5. Jed and Mike have to do the dishes. What does **do the dishes** mean?

   a. Put the dishes in the cupboard.

   b. Wash and dry the dishes.

   c. Put the dishes on the table.

Characters and Actions

6. Mom punished Jon for not feeding Max. What was Jon's punishment?

   a. Jon had to leave the table.

   b. Jon had to wait to eat dinner.

   c. Jon didn't get to play.

7. What did Jon do while his family ate?

   a. Jon thought about playing.

   b. Jon thought about doing the dishes.

   c. Jon thought about his job and how important it was.

8. Mom wanted to teach Jon a lesson. What lesson did she want Jon to learn?

   a. It is important to do your job.

   b. Feeding Max is not important.

   c. Feeding Charlie is fun.

Asking Questions

Ask me a question about Jon's punishment.

Writing Prompt ••

Pretend you are Max. Write a note to Jon. Remind him to feed you.

Story 2

Kit was having a sleepover. The lights were out. Kit and Lu were asleep. Jill was awake. She wasn't sleepy. What was that? She heard something. She sat up in bed. It sounded like someone running on the roof. Jill's heart beat faster and faster. She heard it again. Jill was scared. She flipped the light on.

Jill shook Lu and Kit. "Wake up! Be quiet and listen! I heard something," Jill said. The girls listened. Then they all heard the sound of running feet.

"Did you hear that?" asked Jill.

"Don't worry," said Kit. "That's a family of raccoons. They live in our trees. They run around and play at night. It's okay. We can go back to sleep now. Just don't listen to them," she said.

Main Idea and Details

1. What is the main idea of this story?

    a. Jill got scared when she heard something.

    b. The girls had a birthday party.

    c. Jill didn't want to sleep.

2. What was the noise Jill heard?

    a. The raccoons running across the roof.

    b. The raccoons eating.

    c. The trees brushing on the roof.

3. How did Jill wake up Lu and Kit?

    a. She poked them.

    b. She yelled at them to wake up.

    c. She shook them and said, "Wake up."

Vocabulary and Semantics

4. **Jill flipped the light on.** What does that mean?

    a. She fell over the light.

    b. She turned the light off.

    c. She turned the light on.

5. Jill was scared. What is another word for **scared**?

    a. tired

    b. frightened

    c. unhappy

Characters and Actions

6. What were the raccoons doing on the roof?

    a. The raccoons were running across the roof.

    b. The raccoons were eating.

    c. The raccoons were sleeping.

7. Why was Jill scared?

    a. She was not in her own bed.

    b. She heard something and she didn't know what it was.

    c. She read a scary book.

8. What did Jill do when she got scared?

    a. She got out of bed and looked around.

    b. She covered her eyes.

    c. She turned on the lights and woke up her friends.

Asking Questions

Ask me a question about a sleepover.

Writing Prompt ··

Write about a time you were scared. Describe what happened.

Story 3

Tate had work to do. He wanted to make a gift for his mom. He didn't want his mom to know about the gift. Every day for two weeks, Tate went to his Uncle Bob's house. He used Uncle Bob's tools. Tate was very careful with the saw. He also used a hammer and some nails.

One day Tate's mom came to pick him up at Uncle Bob's. "Come with me. I have something to show you," Tate said. He took her to the workshop. Her gift was covered up with a sheet. "Close your eyes," Tate said. He pulled off the sheet. "Okay, you can look," he said. There was a birdhouse. Tate's mom was so surprised that she cried.

Main Idea and Details

1. What is the main idea of this story?

   a. Tate made a gift for his mom.

   b. Tate liked to go to Uncle Bob's.

   c. Tate was a nice boy.

2. What did Tate use at Uncle Bob's?

   a. a gift

   b. tools

   c. a birdhouse

3. How many weeks did Tate work on his mom's gift?

   a. He worked one week.

   b. He worked two weeks.

   c. He worked three weeks.

Vocabulary and Semantics

4. The story says, "Tate had work to do." What was Tate's work?

   a. Tate was building a birdhouse.

   b. Tate was waiting for his mom.

   c. Tate was sweeping the floor.

Making Inferences and Drawing Conclusions

5. Why didn't Tate want his mom to know about the birdhouse?

   a. He wanted to make it by himself.

   b. He wanted to surprise his mom.

   c. He wanted only Uncle Bob to know about the birdhouse.

Readability 2.5
Copyright © 2005 LinguiSystems, Inc.

Characters and Actions

6. Fill in the blank in this sentence. Tate was very ____ with the saw.

    a. jumpy

    b. hard

    c. careful

7. How did Tate hide the gift?

    a. He put it in a box.

    b. He put it in a garage.

    c. He covered it with a sheet.

8. Why did Tate's mom cry?

    a. because she was happy

    b. because she was sad

    c. because she was angry

Asking Questions

Ask me a question about using tools in a workshop.

> **Writing Prompt** ••
>
> Pretend you are Tate's mom. Write a letter to a friend. Tell the friend about your surprise gift from Tate.

Story 4

Sasha is visiting her grandparents. They live in a house on a horse farm. Grandpa is a horse trainer. He gets horses ready to race. He lets Sasha go with him to the horse barn.

Sasha helps Grandpa feed the horses. Sasha carries oats in a bucket and Grandpa carries bales of hay. They put hay and oats in each feed box.

Grandpa asked Sasha to wait outside one stall. He said, "I have a surprise for you." Soon he opened the door and came out of the stall. He had a colt with him. The colt was light brown. It had a white patch on its forehead. The white patch looked like a star. The colt walked around on its wobbly legs. It swished its tail back and forth.

Sasha was so excited. She ran to the colt and petted it. "What shall we name him?" Grandpa asked.

"I think we should call him Starbright. He has a star on his forehead. He looks frisky, too," Sasha said.

"Starbright it is," said Grandpa, "and he is yours. This is your birthday surprise!" Sasha jumped with joy!

Main Idea and Details

1. What is the main idea of this story?
    a. Sasha likes horses.
    b. Sasha gets a birthday surprise.
    c. Sasha petted a colt.

2. Where do Sasha's grandparents live?
    a. in a cottage
    b. in a village
    c. on a horse farm

3. Where does Sasha put the food for the horses?
    a. in their stalls
    b. in their dishes
    c. in their feed boxes

Vocabulary and Semantics

4. Grandpa is a horse trainer. What is another word for **trainer**?
    a. farmer
    b. teacher
    c. janitor

5. Sasha carries oats for the horse in a bucket. What is another word for **bucket**?
    a. pail
    b. basket
    c. box

6. True or false? The colt had long and steady legs.

Characters and Actions

7. What did Sasha do with the bucket?

    a. She carried oats to the horses in it.

    b. She carried bales of hay with it.

    c. She put it in the stall.

8. What did Grandpa do in the horse stall?

    a. He got the colt.

    b. He got a bale of hay.

    c. He got a feed box.

9. What did Grandpa do for Sasha?

    a. He took her to a movie.

    b. He gave her a birthday surprise.

    c. He showed her a saddle.

Asking Questions

Ask me a question about feeding horses.

Writing Prompt ••

Imagine you are Sasha. Write a thank-you note to Grandpa.

Readability 3.0
Copyright © 2005 LinguiSystems, Inc.

Story 5

Joe, his mom, and Tiger got in the car. They went to see Grandma. Grandma was sitting in her yard waiting for them. The dog from next door was in her lap. Joe opened the door and Tiger jumped out. The dog jumped out of Grandma's lap and barked at Tiger. Tiger took off. Joe followed Tiger.

Tiger ran down the street. Joe ran after him, but he could not catch Tiger. Tiger ran out of sight.

Joe looked and looked for Tiger. He called and called Tiger. Tiger did not come. Joe was sure Tiger was lost. Joe went back to Grandma's house. He was sad. Grandma said, "Don't worry Joe. Tiger will come back."

It was almost time for bed. Joe opened the door to call Tiger one more time. There stood Tiger. Grandma was right!

Main Idea and Details

1. What is the main idea of this story?

   a. Joe's cat runs away.

   b. The family visits Grandma.

   c. Grandma doesn't worry.

2. Where was Grandma when Joe's family got to her house?

   a. at the neighbors' home

   b. sitting in her yard

   c. in her house

3. At the end of the story, where was Tiger?

   a. in a tree

   b. at the neighbors' house

   c. outside Grandma's door

Vocabulary and Semantics

4. **When the dog barked, Tiger took off.** What does that mean?

   a. Tiger ran away after the dog barked.

   b. Tiger took off his paws when he heard the dog.

   c. Tiger jumped after the dog barked.

   d. both *b* and *c*

5. **Tiger ran out of sight**. What does that mean?

   a. Tiger ran as fast as Joe.

   b. Tiger ran so fast, he couldn't see.

   c. Tiger ran too far away to be seen.

Characters and Actions

6. What did the dog do that caused the problem?

    a. He jumped on the cat.

    b. He bit the cat.

    c. He barked at the cat.

7. Grandma predicted what Tiger would do. What was her prediction?

    a. that Tiger would not come back

    b. that Tiger would come back

    c. that Tiger would climb a tree

8. Why was Joe feeling sad?

    a. He thought he wouldn't see Tiger again.

    b. He thought he would have to go to bed.

    c. He didn't know where his mom was.

Asking Questions

Pretend Tiger could talk. Ask him a question about running away.

> **Writing Prompt** ··
>
> Pretend you are Joe. Write a note to your aunt, who lives in another state. Tell her what happened when you went to visit Grandma.

Story 6

Jim lives on a big farm. There is a long, steep hill on the farm called Thrill Hill. It's a good hill to go sledding on. Yesterday there was a big snowstorm. Jim called his friends JT, Marcus, and Cinda to come over and go sledding.

Jim and his friends like to race down Thrill Hill. Jim has some old sleds that go very fast. Jim's sister, Carm, likes to be the starter for the races. She also keeps track of who wins each race. All of the kids got on their sleds. "On your mark. Get set. Go!" yelled Carm. Everyone took off.

Everyone was going very fast. Jim took the lead. Partway down the hill, Jim hit a bump. He wiped out. He flew off his sled and landed in a pile of snow. Cinda zoomed past Jim. JT looked over at Jim and steered into a snowdrift. Marcus sailed by both boys.

Marcus caught up with Cinda. They were neck-and-neck. Cinda was sure she would win. Marcus was sure he would win. Cinda and Marcus stayed side-by-side. Suddenly two rabbits hopped across the hill. They were in the path of Cinda and Marcus. Cinda steered to the right. Marcus steered to the left. Cinda flipped over and rolled and rolled on the snow. Marcus ran into a bank of snow. He got buried in the snow.

The race was over and nobody won. Everyone laughed as they headed back up the hill. They were ready to go again.

Readability 3.5
Copyright © 2005 LinguiSystems, Inc.

Main Idea and Details

1. What is the main idea of this story?

    a. Jim lives on a farm.

    b. Jim and his friends have a sledding race.

    c. Some friends like winter.

2. What is Thrill Hill?

    a. a farm

    b. a long, steep hill

    c. a playground

3. What were the children riding?

    a. toboggans

    b. bikes

    c. sleds

Vocabulary and Semantics

4. **Cinda and Marcus were neck-and-neck in the race.** What does that mean?

    a. They were even in the race.

    b. They had their necks sticking out.

    c. They had their necks near each other.

5. In the story, **Jim wiped out**. What does that mean?

    a. He wiped snow off his face.

    b. He was sad he lost and wiped his tears away.

    c. He crashed his sled and was out of the race.

6. True or false? A **snowdrift** is a place that makes snow in the winter.

Characters and Actions

7. What did Cinda and Marcus do when they saw the rabbits?

   a. They yelled at the rabbits to move.

   b. They steered away from the rabbits.

   c. They stopped so the rabbits could cross the hill.

8. What did Cinda and Marcus do that ended the race?

   a. Cinda flipped over and Marcus ran into a snowbank.

   b. Cinda got off her sled and Marcus turned over on his sled.

   c. Cinda leaned back on her sled to slow down and Marcus jumped off his sled.

9. What happened to Marcus when he hit the snowbank?

   a. He got buried in the snow.

   b. He ran through the snow.

   c. He cried because he was sad.

Asking Questions

Ask me a question about snowdrifts.

Writing Prompt ··

Write a different ending for this story.

Story 7

Every month someone at our house is "Star for a Day." This month my sister Leah is the "Star." She chooses the food we eat for dinner. She helps plan the meal. She gets to set the table. Then she helps cook the meal.

Everyone in the family writes a note to the "Star." The note says what makes the "Star" special. After supper, "Star for a Day" reads the notes out loud. Then everyone helps clear the table. Everyone also cleans up the kitchen.

Then Leah gets to choose something for the family to do. The family might go swimming or to a movie. They might get to play golf or go to a park. They might have popcorn or a hot fudge sundae. It's fun to be "Star for a Day" at our house!

Main Idea and Details

1. What is the main idea of this story?

    a. The "Star for a Day" gets to do special things.

    b. Everyone can be a "Star for a Day."

    c. The "Star for a Day" gets popcorn.

2. Who writes notes to the "Star for a Day"?

    a. the "Star's" teacher

    b. the "Star's" friends

    c. everyone in the "Star's" family

3. What meal does the "Star" get to choose?

    a. breakfast

    b. lunch

    c. dinner

Vocabulary and Semantics

4. In the story, **everyone helps clear the table**. What does that mean?

    a. Family members put the dishes on the table.

    b. Family members remove the dishes from the table.

    c. Family members put food on the table.

5. The "Star" reads the notes out loud. What is another word for **notes**?

    a. words

    b. messages

    c. papers

6. True or false? **Sundae** is the day after Saturday.

Characters and Actions

7. When everyone cleans up the kitchen, what do they do?

   a. wash the windows and vacuum the walls

   b. put the food away, wash the dishes, and straighten up the kitchen

   c. set the table and put the food on

8. Before planning the dinner, what does the "Star" have to do?

   a. set the table

   b. choose the food

   c. shop for the food

9. What does everyone tell the "Star" in the notes they write?

   a. what they want to do with the "Star"

   b. what they want for dinner

   c. what they think makes the "Star" special

Asking Questions

Ask me a question about what it would be like to be "Star for a Day" at school.

Writing Prompt ••

Pretend your mother is "Star for a Day." Write a note to her telling what makes her special.

Story 8

I like to visit Aunt June. She lives on a farm and grows all of her own food. She cans tomatoes, carrots, beans, and corn. Sometimes she sells her food at a farmers' market.

Sometimes I help Aunt June make tomato juice. We cook the tomatoes in a big kettle on the stove. Then we squeeze out the juice. One time we made ten quarts of tomato juice.

My dog, Tippy, likes to play with Aunt June's collie, Jake. They got in trouble last week. Tippy and Jake chased some rabbits into the woods. Later the dogs showed up at the back door. We couldn't let them in because they smelled putrid. Somewhere the dogs had encountered a skunk. They got too close to it and got sprayed. It was gross. They smelled awful.

Aunt June said, "The only way to get rid of the odor is to bathe the dogs in tomato juice."

After his tomato juice bath, Tippy shook his coat. He splattered tomato juice all over me. Jake did exactly the same thing. What a mess! At least the dogs didn't stink anymore. Thank goodness for Aunt June's tomato juice!

Main Idea and Details

1. What is the main idea of this story?

    a. Jessie's visit to Aunt June's

    b. Jessie has a dog named Tippy.

    c. Tippy likes to play with Jake.

2. In what state does the story take place?

    a. The story doesn't tell.

    b. on a farm in Wisconsin

    c. in a city in Wisconsin

3. What happened to the dogs?

    a. They ran away for two days.

    b. They got sprayed by a skunk.

    c. They drank tomato juice.

Vocabulary and Semantics

4. The dogs smelled putrid. What is another word for **putrid**?

    a. terrible or horrible

    b. dreadful or unpleasant

    c. awful

    d. all of the above

5. The dogs encountered a skunk. What does **encountered** mean?

    a. met unexpectedly

    b. heard in the distance

    c. smelled

6. True or false? Another word for **scent** is **odor**.

Readability 4.0
Copyright © 2005 LinguiSystems, Inc.

Characters and Actions

7. Which statement is true about Aunt June?
   a. She enjoys hunting for her food.
   b. She doesn't like dogs because they stink.
   c. She likes to raise vegetables.

8. What does Aunt June do with extra food she grows?
   a. She feeds it to wild animals.
   b. She sells it at a farmers' market.
   c. both *a* and *b*

9. Why did Aunt June suggest bathing the dogs in tomato juice?
   a. She wanted to use up her tomato juice before it spoiled.
   b. She was trying to save her water.
   c. She knew only tomato juice would get rid of the skunk odor.

Asking Questions

Ask me a question about what it would be like to live on a farm.

Writing Prompt ··

Pretend Aunt June has invited you and a friend to spend a day on her farm. Write to her to tell her what you hope to do while you are visiting her farm.

Story 9

During dinner JD announced, "I'm not feeling very well. My stomach feels funny and my nose is runny." JD's dad patted him on the head and said, "I bet you've got a case of butterflies. Hurry now because we need to leave soon."

When JD got to school, he went straight to his classroom. As he headed down the hall, Grandma yelled, "Break a leg, JD!" Then Grandma, Dad, and JD's sister went to the gym to find seats for the concert.

JD and his class came on stage and filed onto the risers. Partway through the first song, JD's best friend, Ned, fainted. Mr. Lawton, the principal, was backstage. He rushed out and carried Ned offstage.

Miss Smith, the music teacher, calmly asked the students to look at her. Then she said, "Smile. Remember, the show must go on." The students started singing again.

JD still felt funny. Suddenly he sneezed. Then he sneezed again and keeled over. Mr. Lawton escorted JD to the nurse's office. He said, "You're burning up, JD. You have red spots on your face and arms. You and Ned have some of the same symptoms. I'll get Nurse Jones to look at you two. I know she's in the audience," said Mr. Lawton.

Nurse Jones came to her office. She took the boys' temperatures. "I think you boys have the measles," she said. "You have the symptoms: a temperature, a runny nose, red eyes, and a skin rash. Measles is contagious. I must alert your classmates' parents because they will need to watch for symptoms."

"Well," JD said. "I'd rather have a case of measles than a case of butterflies!"

Main Idea and Details

1. What event was going on at the school?

    a. a variety show

    b. a science fair

    c. a concert

2. Who fainted during the concert?

    a. JD and Grandpa

    b. Ned and JD

    c. Ned and JD's sister

3. What were JD's symptoms?

    a. a fever

    b. a runny nose and red eyes

    c. a rash on his skin

    d. all of the above

Vocabulary and Semantics

4. **JD had red spots on his skin.** What is another way to say that?

    a. He had knobs on his skin.

    b. He had a skin rash.

    c. He had blisters on his skin.

5. **JD was burning up.** What does that mean?

    a. JD felt hot.

    b. JD had a fever.

    c. both *a* and *b*

6. True or false? Something **contagious** can easily spread to other people.

Characters and Actions

7. What did the principal ask the nurse to do?

    a. to listen to the concert

    b. to call the boys' parents

    c. to examine the boys

8. After JD keeled over, what did the principal do?

    a. removed JD from the stage

    b. waved something smelly under JD's nose

    c. took JD to the school office

    d. both *a* and *c*

9. What did the nurse do with the thermometer?

    a. checked the boys' ears

    b. checked the boys' temperatures

    c. checked the boys' throats

Asking Questions

Ask me a question about measles.

Writing Prompt ··

Pretend you are the nurse. Write a note to the parents of JD's classmates telling them about measles in the school.

Spotlight on Reading Comprehension:
Characters and Actions

33

Readability 4.0
Copyright © 2005 LinguiSystems, Inc.

Story 10

Jake jumped on his bike and headed to his grandpa's house. Jake and his grandpa were going fishing. Jake likes to be with his grandpa. Grandpa tells him funny stories and plays games with him. Grandpa also is a good fisherman. He always catches lots of fish and then he cooks them. Grandpa probably cooks fish better than anyone in the whole world.

Grandpa has a big tackle box. He keeps fishing lures and hooks in it. Sometimes Grandpa uses night crawlers or minnows to catch fish. Grandpa stores his bait in an old refrigerator in the garage.

Last night Jake helped Grandpa gather night crawlers. They needed a fresh supply of bait. After dark when it was raining, Jake and Grandpa went outside. They took their flashlights. They shined the lights on the ground. They saw gobs of night crawlers lying on the grass. Grandpa started to pick up the worms. He put them into coffee cans that had been filled with damp dirt.

Jake tried to pick up a worm. It squirmed and wiggled. Two worms tried to go back in the ground. Jake pulled too hard on one worm, so it broke in half. Grandpa said that was okay because it would still be good bait. Jake put the broken worm in a coffee can.

Now Jake can hardly wait to go fishing. He knows he and Grandpa will come home with a full stringer of fish. After they clean the fish, he knows he and Grandpa will have a great dinner!

Readability 4.1

Main Idea and Details

1. What is the main idea of this story?

   a. Jake has a grandpa.

   b. Jake and his grandpa got night crawlers for fishing.

   c. Jake likes to ride his bike.

2. Where does Grandpa keep his night crawlers?

   a. in his tackle box

   b. in the ground

   c. in an old refrigerator

3. Where did Jake and his grandpa find their night crawlers?

   a. at the bait shop

   b. in Grandpa's yard

   c. in the refrigerator

Vocabulary and Semantics

4. Jake was **headed to** Grandpa's. What does that mean?

   a. Jake was going to Grandpa's.

   b. Jake was ahead of Grandpa.

   c. Jake was standing near Grandpa.

5. Jake and Grandpa saw **gobs of night crawlers**. What is another way to say that?

   a. They saw many earthworms.

   b. They saw a few earthworms.

6. True or false? A **tackle box** is a container for storing things you need when you play football.

Characters and Actions

7. When Jake tried to pick up the earthworms, what did they do?
   a. They squirmed and tried to go back into the ground.
   b. They squealed and crawled away.
   c. They curled up.

8. How do we know Grandpa is a good fisherman?
   a. He hunts for night crawlers when it's raining.
   b. He catches a lot of fish.
   c. He cooks fish well.

9. What does Grandpa do with the fish he catches?
   a. He throws them back in the water.
   b. He cleans them, cooks them, and eats them.
   c. He gives them away.

Asking Questions

Ask me a question about a stringer of fish.

Writing Prompt ••

Pretend you are Jake. Write a letter to your cousin describing how you gathered night crawlers with Grandpa.

Story 11

Every day after school, Sarah gets her wagon. She pulls it to the curb in front of her house. She loads a bundle of newspapers into the wagon. She pulls the wagon to deliver her papers. Sarah has thirty customers. Mrs. Bud is her oldest customer. She is eighty.

Mrs. Bud always comes to the door with Tag, her dog, to get the paper. Yesterday Mrs. Bud didn't come to the door. Tag came to the door. He barked and barked. Sarah talked to Tag from the porch. Tag usually stops barking. He kept barking. Sarah rang the doorbell. Mrs. Bud still didn't answer the door. Sarah left the paper on the porch. Then she finished her route.

Sarah was worried about Mrs. Bud. She told her mother what had happened. Sarah wanted to go check on Mrs. Bud. Sarah and her mother found Mrs. Bud lying on her kitchen floor. Mrs. Bud had fallen and couldn't get up. Sarah held Mrs. Bud's hand and her mother called 911. They didn't move Mrs. Bud. They all waited for the EMTs.

Because of Sarah's good deed, Mrs. Bud will get well. The newspaper put Sarah's picture on the front page. The headline said, "Papergirl Saves Elderly Woman."

Main Idea and Details

1. What is the main idea of this story?

   a. Sarah likes her paper route.

   b. Sarah delivers newspapers.

   c. Sarah thought something was wrong and did something about it.

2. Who is Sarah's oldest customer?

   a. The story doesn't tell.

   b. Mrs. Bud

   c. Sarah's next-door neighbor

3. What was in the newspaper?

   a. a picture of Mrs. Bud and Tag

   b. a picture of Sarah and her mother

   c. a picture of Sarah

Vocabulary and Semantics

4. Sarah picks up her newspapers at the curb in front of her house. What is a **curb**?

   a. the edge of the street

   b. the sidewalk

   c. the driveway

5. Sarah loaded a bundle of papers into her wagon. What is a **bundle of papers**?

   a. a carton of papers

   b. a sack full of papers

   c. a stack of papers tied together

6. Sarah wanted to check on Mrs. Bud. What does **check on** mean in this story?

   a. Sarah wanted to see if Mrs. Bud was okay.

   b. Sarah wanted to spy on Mrs. Bud.

Characters and Actions

7. What does Mrs. Bud usually do when Sarah delivers the paper?

   a. She comes to the door.

   b. She gets the paper from the mailbox.

   c. She lets Tag get the paper.

8. When Mrs. Bud didn't answer the door, what did Tag do that probably made Sarah think something was wrong?

   a. He kept barking.

   b. He jumped up and down.

   c. He didn't do anything.

9. How did the newspaper honor Sarah for her good deed?

   a. They gave her a reward.

   b. They put her picture on the front page.

   c. They gave her a vacation.

Asking Questions

Ask me a question about Mrs. Bud.

Writing Prompt ••

Pretend you are Mrs. Bud. Write a letter to the editor of the newspaper telling about Sarah.

Answer Key

Story 1
1. a
2. c
3. b
4. c
5. b
6. b
7. c
8. a

Story 2
1. a
2. a
3. c
4. c
5. b
6. a
7. b
8. c

Story 3
1. a
2. b
3. b
4. a
5. b
6. c
7. c
8. a

Story 4
1. b
2. c
3. c
4. b
5. a
6. false
7. a
8. a
9. b

Story 5
1. a
2. b
3. c
4. a
5. c
6. c
7. b
8. a

Story 6
1. b
2. b
3. c
4. a
5. c
6. false
7. b
8. a
9. a

Story 7
1. a
2. c
3. c
4. b
5. b
6. false
7. b
8. b
9. c

Story 8
1. a
2. a
3. b
4. d
5. a
6. true
7. c
8. b
9. c

Story 9
1. c
2. b
3. d
4. b
5. c
6. true
7. c
8. d
9. b

Story 10
1. b
2. c
3. b
4. a
5. a
6. false
7. a
8. b
9. b

Story 11
1. c
2. b
3. c
4. a
5. c
6. a
7. a
8. a
9. b

23-05-9876543